SCIENTIFIC AMERICAN | EDUCATIONAL PUBLISHING

SCIENTIFIC AMERICAN INVESTIGATES CAREERS IN SCIENCE

MARINE BIOLOGIST

BY MEGAN QUICK

Published in 2026 by The Rosen Publishing Group
in association with Scientific American Educational Publishing
2544 Clinton Street, Buffalo NY 14224

Copyright © 2026 Rosen Publishing Group

Library of Congress Cataloging-in-Publication Data
Names: Quick, Megan author
Title: Marine biologist / Megan Quick.
Description: Buffalo, New York : Scientific American Educational Publishing, an imprint of Rosen Publishing, [2026] | Series: Scientific American investigates careers in science | "Portions of this work were originally authored by Zelda Salt and published as Be a Marine Biologist. All new material in this edition is authored by Megan Quick."
| Includes bibliographical references and index. | Audience term: juvenile | Audience: Grades 4-6 Scientific American Educational Publishing, an imprint of Rosen Publishing
Identifiers: LCCN 2025002105 (print) | LCCN 2025002106 (ebook) | ISBN 9781725352599 (library binding) | ISBN 9781725352582 (paperback) | ISBN 9781725352605 (ebook)
Subjects: LCSH: Marine biologists–Juvenile literature | Aquatic biology–Vocational guidance–Juvenile literature | Marine sciences–Vocational guidance–Juvenile literature
Classification: LCC QH91.45 .Q53 2026 (print) | LCC QH91.45 (ebook) | DDC 578.77023–dc23/eng/20250211
LC record available at https://lccn.loc.gov/2025002105
LC ebook record available at https://lccn.loc.gov/2025002106

Designer: Leslie Taylor
Editor: Megan Quick

Portions of this work were originally authored by Zelda Salt and published as *Be a Marine Biologist*. All new material in this edition is authored by Megan Quick.

Photo credits: Cover (main) Nicole Helgason/Shutterstock.com; series art (background) jijomathaidesigners/Shutterstock.com; p. 5 Nicholas J Klein/Shutterstock.com; p. 7 (layers) LukaSkywalker/Shutterstock.com, (corals) silvae/Shutterstock.com; p. 9 Zacarias da Mata/Shutterstock.com; p. 10 Madelein Wolfaardt/Shutterstock.com; p. 11 Ryan Sleiman/Shutterstock.com; p. 13 Willyam Bradberry/Shutterstock.com; p. 15 KARI K/Shutterstock.com; p. 17 Stas Makes Content/Shutterstock.com; p. 18 Alexandre.ROSA/Shutterstock.com; p. 19 AZ Septian/Shutterstock.com; p. 20 U.S. Fish and Wildlife Service/File:Rachel-Carson.jpg_commons.wikimedia.org; p. 21 U.S. Fish and Wildlife Service/ File:Rachel Carson Conducts Marine Biology Research with Bob Hines.jpg_commons.wikimedia.org; p. 23 divedog/Shutterstock.com; p. 25 Kryvenok Anastasiia/Shutterstock.com; p. 27 Imfoto/Shutterstock.com; p. 29 Rainer von Brandis/iStockphoto.com.

Some of the images in this book illustrate individuals who are models. The depictions do not imply actual situations or events.

All rights reserved. No part of this book may be reproduced in any form without permission in writing from the publisher, except by a reviewer.

Printed in the United States of America

CPSIA compliance information: Batch #CSSA26. For Further Information contact Rosen Publishing at 1-800-237-9932.

CONTENTS

SEA OF LIFE 4
UNDERWATER WORLDS 6
FISH AND FRIENDS 8
DEEP DIVING 10
MAMMALS AT SEA 12
TRAINING AND TEACHING 14
PROTECTING MARINE LIFE 16
FIGHTING POLLUTION 18
SEALIFE HELPING HUMANS 22
TECH SUPPORT 24
SCHOOL DAYS 26
GET STARTED! 28
GLOSSARY 30
FOR MORE INFORMATION 31
INDEX 32

Words in the glossary appear in **bold** type the first time they are used in the text.

SEA OF LIFE

When you think of the ocean, you may picture fish, dolphins, or sharks. But did you know that there are more than 240,000 known **species** in the sea? And there are many more that haven't been discovered yet. Only a small part of the ocean has ever been explored.

Marine biologists study life in the ocean. This includes everything from tiny organisms that can only be seen with a **microscope**, to the blue whale, the largest animal in the sea. Marine biologists also study the ocean's plant life and **ecosystems**. There is a lot to explore if you choose a career as a marine biologist.

FUN FACT

SCIENTISTS BELIEVE THAT ABOUT 90 PERCENT OF LIFE IN THE OCEAN HAS NOT YET BEEN DISCOVERED. BUT THEY ARE MAKING PROGRESS! AN AVERAGE OF ABOUT 2,300 NEW SPECIES ARE FOUND EACH YEAR.

About 71 percent of the world is water, and most of that is marine water, or salt water.

UNDERWATER WORLDS

The ocean is full of ecosystems that include animal and plant life as well as features such as tall mountains and deep **trenches**. Ecosystems may be deep under the surface, near the shore, or out in open waters. Marine biologists are interested in learning how animals and plants in the ocean **interact** with each other as well as the **environment**.

Each type of ecosystem has different conditions and is suited to certain populations. Sunny coral **reefs** are full of species that each play a role in keeping the reef healthy and balanced. In the deep sea, there are fewer species, and those have adapted to living with little sunlight.

FUN FACT

CORALS MAY LOOK LIKE COLORFUL PLANTS, BUT THEY ARE SEA ANIMALS. CORALS INCLUDE MANY TINY ANIMALS CALLED POLYPS. MOST CORALS LIVE IN GROUPS, OR COLONIES. THEY FEED ON SMALL FISH OR TINY LIFEFORMS CALLED PLANKTON.

Marine Animals: Where They Live

Each zone shown here represents an ocean depth, or deepness, where different marine animals live. Most animals that we know of live closer to the surface.

FISH AND FRIENDS

Marine biologists who study fish species, which include sharks and stingrays, are called ichthyologists. They observe how fish behave, how they have changed over time, and how they have adapted to their environment.

Ichthyologists may identify different types of fish, check water quality, or study data. Most do not spend a lot of their time in the ocean. Instead, they might work at laboratories or **aquariums**. The aquariums contain large tanks that have been set up with conditions like those in the ocean. Scientists are able to see how the marine life behaves just like they would in their natural ecosystem.

FUN FACT

SHARKS ARE FISH! THEY USE FINS TO MOVE THROUGH THE WATER AND THEY BREATHE THROUGH GILLS, WHICH ARE SLITS IN THEIR SIDES THAT ALLOW THEM TO TAKE IN OXYGEN FROM THE WATER.

These marine biologists work at a large aquarium where they swim in tanks to study fish and other sea life.

DEEP DIVING

Ichthyologists who study fish in their natural environment are often scuba certified. This means that they've learned how to use special equipment to breathe underwater. The first part of training happens in the classroom. The scuba student learns what each piece of scuba equipment does, what signals divers use to talk to each other underwater, and what goes into planning a dive.

Once they've learned the basics, the student spends time practicing in a pool. They'll put on the gear and get comfortable moving underwater. Finally, they go on a couple of open dives with an instructor. The student must pass a final test before they are scuba certified.

Scuba divers carry a tank of oxygen on their back that allows them to breathe underwater.

MAMMALS AT SEA

The ocean isn't just full of fish! There are plenty of **mammals** as well. A marine mammalogist studies animals such as seals, dolphins, and even polar bears. They learn about the animals and their behaviors, environment, and how they've changed and adapted over time. They may track mammals to observe how and where they move throughout the ocean.

As with most scientists, mammalogists choose a **specialty**. They may focus on a species, such as pinnipeds, which includes seals, sea lions, and walruses. Or they might study the marine mammals in a certain environment, such as a polar area, or an island far in the ocean.

FUN FACT

YOU MIGHT BE SURPRISED TO FIND A BEAR ON THE LIST OF MARINE MAMMALS! POLAR BEARS SPEND MOST OF THEIR TIME ON ARCTIC ICE AND THEY GET THEIR FOOD FROM THE OCEAN. THEY'RE ALSO GREAT SWIMMERS.

Dolphins can stay underwater for a long time, but they must come to the surface to breathe.

Top of Their Class

Dolphins are probably the smartest animals in the sea, and marine mammalogists have spent a lot of time studying their behaviors. Dolphins live in groups and speak to each other with their own language of clicks and squeaks. Scientists have found that they are quick learners and are caring, creative, and playful.

TRAINIING AND TEACHING

Have you been to a zoo and seen a trainer working with an animal? Zoos and aquariums often hire marine biologists as their animal trainers and handlers. Many trainers have a degree in marine biology, with a focus on animal behavior. They might work with seals, dolphins, or whales.

Sometimes public speaking is involved with being an animal trainer. Many trainers perform demonstrations, or shows, for zoo and aquarium visitors.

Trainers do their best to treat their animals with care. However, not all marine mammals do well living in tanks. Orcas in the wild, for example, travel more than 62 miles (100 km) per day. They can't swim nearly that far in a tank!

Trainers feed and care for the animals they train. Here, a trainer brushes a harbor seal's teeth.

Inventor of the Aquarium

In 1832, a French scientist named Jeanne Villepreux-Power wanted to learn more about a special type of octopus. At that time, the only way to study sea animals was when they were dead. Villepreux-Power invented the glass aquarium so that she could observe the animal's behavior and **physical** features.

PROTECTING MARINE LIFE

Many marine biologists work to find ways of keeping marine life safe and healthy. One danger facing fish today is overfishing. This happens when too many adult fish are caught, and the population of fish has trouble surviving. Overfishing threatens many populations of fish species, such as the bluefin tuna.

People around the world depend on fish as a food source. Fishing is a big business that brings in a lot of money. Marine biologists who work in fisheries science focus on how humans and sea life can live together, balancing our need for food with keeping marine ecosystems healthy. This means tracking fish populations, protecting at-risk areas, and educating the public.

Workers on this large fishing boat are hauling in a big net of fish.

17

FIGHTING POLLUTION

Overfishing is just one of many problems facing the world's oceans and the life they contain. Scientists are always looking for ways to undo the harm that humans have done to the environment. Marine biologists play an important part in this work.

One example is the work being done to help the Great Barrier Reef in Australia. Once one of the most **diverse** areas of the world, the coral there has been dying at a high rate, in part thanks to pollution. Scientists are growing healthy baby corals in tanks and pools, and then placing them in the damaged reefs.

Great Barrier Reef

Marine Food Web

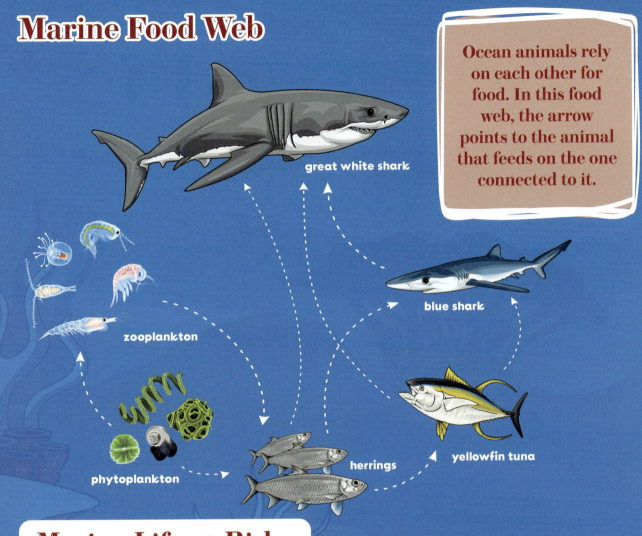

Ocean animals rely on each other for food. In this food web, the arrow points to the animal that feeds on the one connected to it.

Marine Life at Risk

A 2024 study states that if **climate change** continues to cause ocean waters to warm, a key group of sea animals could become extinct, or die out. Plankton are tiny lifeforms that are an important part of the ocean food web. If they become extinct, it would affect all marine life that depend on them to live.

Some marine biologists have taken on the job of sounding the alarm about the dangers of pollution to ocean ecosystems. They might talk in courts about oil spills, illegal fishing, and other human-made disasters.

One well-known example is marine biologist Rachel Carson. She wrote four books in her lifetime, including three books about the ocean: *Under the Sea Wind*, *The Sea Around Us*, and *The Edge of the Sea*. These three books celebrated, or honored, the diverse life in the ocean. Carson's writing detailed the science of the ocean and what life is like for different creatures that live underwater.

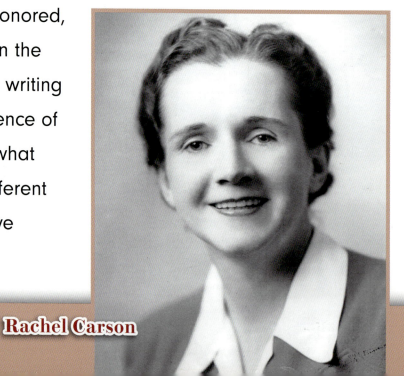

Rachel Carson

Rachel Carson

FUN FACT

EACH YEAR, PEOPLE DUMP AS MUCH AS 13.2 MILLION TONS (12 MILLION MT) OF PLASTIC INTO THE OCEAN. PLASTIC IS ESPECIALLY DANGEROUS BECAUSE WHEN IT BREAKS DOWN IT CAN BE EATEN BY MARINE ANIMALS.

This photo shows Rachel Carson and another scientist studying marine life in the Atlantic Ocean.

SEALIFE HELPING HUMANS

While some marine biologists look for ways to save marine life, others are searching for ways that marine life can help people. Biotechnology is a branch of biology that focuses on using living things to make useful products.

Marine biologists specializing in biotechnology are researching ways that macroalgae, also known as seaweed, can be used to create pollution-free fuel. The macroalgae grow quickly, are inexpensive, and could provide a key source of renewable energy. With so many species in the ocean, scientists are hopeful that they will uncover more ways to use marine life to help the planet.

FUN FACT

RENEWABLE ENERGY COMES FROM SOURCES THAT WILL NOT RUN OUT, OR ARE EASY TO RENEW. COMMON FORMS OF RENEWABLE ENERGY ARE THE SUN, WIND, AND WATER.

The ocean is full of seaweed, seen here, which may be used to create fuel that's not harmful for the environment.

TECH SUPPORT

Like most scientists, marine biologists use technology to assist them in many areas of their work. This technology is constantly improving and changing. Marine biologists use advanced computers and microscopes to study life in the ocean. Some even use deep-sea robots to reach places far down in the ocean.

Marine biologists also used manned submersibles, or vehicles that can go underwater, to explore places no other humans can go. The deepest anyone has ever traveled underwater was 35,756 feet (10,898 m) deep!

Not all tools are advanced technology. For hundreds of years, marine biologists have been using buckets and trawls, or nets dragged behind boats, to collect ocean samples.

This underwater drone explores marine life on the ocean floor. It is operated by a person above water.

Robot Fish

Scientists have created underwater robots that can help with underwater research. One recent example is Belle, a robot fish with a water-powered fin that allows it to swim quietly and blend in with real fish. It contains a camera and collects data and samples as it moves. This exciting technology provides information about marine animals and their ecosystems.

SCHOOL DAYS

Does a career in marine biology sound like a good fit for you? It's never too early to start getting ready. Different marine biology jobs need different levels of schooling, but to become a marine biologist, you will need a bachelor's, or four-year, degree. This could be in a field such as ecology, molecular biology, or zoology. Many marine biologists have advanced degrees, which means they continue with their schooling after they finish at a four-year college.

The name of the degree may be less important than the skills you gain! A marine biologist must be able to communicate well, work with large amounts of data, or information, and solve problems.

Some college classes offer hands-on experience. These students are on a field trip to study marine life.

GET STARTED!

Your career as a marine biologist may be years away, but there are things you can do now to prepare. Visit an aquarium or zoo. Join a club (or start your own) with others interested in ocean life. Check out at-home science kits that allow you to dissect, or cut up, fish to learn more about them. And of course, read lots of books about marine life and ecosystems!

There is so much that we still need to learn about life in the ocean. As a marine biologist, you might discover a new type of sea animal or protect a species in danger. If this is the career for you, go ahead and dive in!

This marine biologist is collecting information about the health of coral reefs.

Sweeping the Beach

Polluted beaches are harmful to marine life. If you are lucky enough to live near (or visit) a beach, find out if you can join a beach sweep. These events are held in many coastal areas, and bring groups of people together to clean up beaches. It's a great way to help protect ocean life.

GLOSSARY

aquarium: A place people can go to see fish and other water animals.

climate change: Long-term change in Earth's climate, caused mainly by human activities such as burning oil and natural gas.

diverse: Differing from each other.

ecosystem: All the living things in an area.

environment: The conditions that surround a living thing and affect the way it lives.

interact: To act on one another.

mammal: A warm-blooded animal that has a backbone and hair, breathes air, and feeds milk to its young.

microscope: A tool used to view very small objects so they can be seen much larger and more clearly.

physical: Having to do with the body.

reef: A chain of rocks or coral, or a ridge of sand, at or near the water's surface.

specialty: A subject or area that a person knows a great deal about.

species: A group of plants or animals that are all of the same kind.

trench: A long, narrow hole in the ground.

FOR MORE INFORMATION

Books

Barr, Catherine. *The World's Wildest Waters: Protecting Life in Seas, Rivers, and Lakes.* New York, NY: DK Publishing, 2023.

Owings, Lisa. *Marine Biologist.* Minneapolis, MN: Bellwether Media, 2024.

Pattison, Darcy. *Aquarium: How Jeannette Power Invented Aquariums to Observe Marine Life.* Little Rock, AR: Mims House Books, 2023.

Websites

American Museum of Natural History
www.amnh.org/explore/ology/marine-biology
Explore the world of marine biology through games, videos, and activities.

National Geographic Kids
www.natgeokids.com/ie/category/discover/animals/sea-life/
Learn fun facts about a variety of marine animals.

Wonderopolis
www.wonderopolis.org/wonder/what-does-a-marine-biologist-do
Discover more about what it's like to be a marine biologist.

Publisher's note to educators and parents: Our editors have carefully reviewed these websites to ensure that they are suitable for students. Many websites change frequently, however, and we cannot guarantee that a site's future contents will continue to meet our high standards of quality and educational value. Be advised that students should be closely supervised whenever they access the internet.

INDEX

animal trainers, 14, 15

aquarium, 8, 9, 14, 15, 28

biotechnology, 22

Carson, Rachel, 20, 21

coral reef, 6, 18, 29

dolphins, 4, 12, 13, 14

ecosystem, 4, 6, 8, 16, 20, 25, 28

fish, 6, 8, 9, 10, 12, 16, 17, 25, 28

fisheries science, 16

Great Barrier Reef, 18

ichthyologists, 8, 10

marine mammologist, 12, 13

microscope, 4, 24

ocean zones, 7

overfishing, 16, 18

plankton, 6, 19

pollution, 18, 20, 22, 29

robot, 24, 25

schooling, 26, 27

scuba diving, 10, 11

seal, 12, 14, 15

shark, 4, 8

submersibles, 24

Villepreux-Power, Jeanne, 15

zoo, 14, 28